Tina Turner

by D.L. Mabery

Lerner Publications Company
Minneapolis

Photo Credits
Warner Brothers, pp. 2, 10, 48; Paul Cox/London Features International, p. 6; Michael Ochs Archives, pp. 14, 16, 20, 24; SL/Retna, p. 30; David Redfern/Retna, p. 34; Harrison Funk/Retna, p. 38; John Bellissimo/Retna, p. 40; Larry Busacca/Retna, pp. 1, 44, 46

Front cover photo by Paul Cox/London Features International
Back cover photo by US/EA/London Features International

Manufactured in the United States of America

LIBRARY OF CONGRESS CATALOGING-IN-PUBLICATION DATA

Mabery, D.L.
 Tina Turner.

 Summary: A biography emphasizing the career of the enduring rock star who received three Grammy Awards in 1985.
  1. Turner, Tina—Juvenile literature. 2. Rock musicians—United States—Biography—Juvenile literature. [1. Turner, Tina. 2. Singers. 3. Rock Music] I. Title.
 ML3930.T87M3 1986   784.5′4′00924 [92]   85-24076
 ISBN 0-8225-1609-8

 1 2 3 4 5 6 7 8 9 10 96 95 94 93 92 91 90 89 88 87 86

CONTENTS

TOTAL CONTROL

When Tina Turner performs, she is a bundle of energy released like a strong, hot wind that sweeps up from the south on a summer evening. With a series of high-kick steps she approaches the microphone and grabs the stand. Tina has that certain authority which can only belong to a performer who has been on stage most of her life. Her characteristic voice is emotional, rough and ragged, as she belts out a song from her multi-platinum

Private Dancer album. "You better *be*…good to *me*," the electrifying singer warns. And the crowd packed into the stadium responds with loud cheers while reaching out toward the stage.

As Tina shimmies about the stage in her high heels, she bobs her head so that her massive mane of streaked hair flails in constant motion. Standing five foot four inches tall and being in the excellent physical condition of a serious athlete, Tina is in total control of the stage and of her show. In fact, Tina's life history is a story about gaining control.

In 1985 Tina was honored by the Academy of Music when she was voted recipient of three Grammy Awards, the highest compliment a person in the musical industry can receive. Tina Turner's *Private Dancer* album was picked as the Best Rock Performance by a Female, Best Pop Performance by a Female, and the Best Record of the Year. It beat such stiff competition as Prince, Lionel Richie, Cyndi Lauper, and Bruce Springsteen.

Winning these Grammy Awards meant more to Tina than simply being honored as a singer who had not had a record album on the market in over five years. Tina Turner's three Grammy Awards symbolized her strength to survive a bad marriage and a broken career. By winning the awards, Tina became an example to everyone everywhere that success could be achieved if one thought positively. The Grammy Awards ceremony honored Tina's spirit as much as it did her music.

Music, as it happens, has also been a way for Tina Turner to open the doors on another of her lifelong dreams: to be an actress.

I MIGHT HAVE BEEN QUEEN

Tina Turner's story began back in a small Tennessee town called Nutbush, located about fifty miles west of Memphis. It was in Nutbush that Floyd Bullock, a devoutly religious Baptist, managed a sharecropper farm for a white plantation boss. His wife, Zelma, half Cherokee Indian, gave birth to the couple's second and last child on November 26, 1939. The little girl was named Anna Mae Bullock, a name she would be known by until she started recording hit singles in the early sixties.

Like her older sister Eileen, Anna Mae grew up picking cotton and fruit in the farmlands that surrounded the dusty streets of Nutbush. Although the Bullock family worked in the fields, their lives were not as hard as those of other families in the tiny town. "We always had nice furniture, and our house was always nice," Tina remembers. "We had our own separate bedroom and a dining room, and we had pigs and animals. I knew people who didn't, so I knew the difference, and we weren't poor."

Little Anna Mae stayed pretty much to herself until she was old enough to go to school. Although she played alone, she was rather adventurous. And she loved the movies. Every chance she would get, Anna Mae would put on some of her mother's housedresses and jewelry. "I would put a bedspread out on the front lawn and lay there, pretending that I was a movie star," Tina said on a television interview.

Anna Mae's reading, writing and arithmetic education came by way of a two-room grammar school, while her understanding of music came from a number of sources. Having inherited her mother's robust singing voice, Anna Mae enjoyed the Sunday sessions singing with the Baptist choir. There were also community picnics where Anna Mae got the opportunity to sing. Everyone brought homebaked goods to share, and there was usually good-time dance music played by local musicians. This music prompted the little Anna Mae to sing and dance along whenever she could.

Of course, there was also music on the radio to inspire the big voice of the little girl. In Tennessee, most of the music on the radio was country music coming from Nashville, but Anna Mae also heard the traditional Delta blues of the black artists such as Muddy Waters, Howlin' Wolf, Bobby "Blue" Bland, and the performer considered to be the main blues man of them all, B. B. King.

In the early years, Tina Turner remembers, she was always singing — singing around the house and singing in the fields as she picked cotton and fruit. Although she didn't understand it at the time, there was a spirit and a feeling in music which communicated directly to her. Later she would learn how to communicate that feeling to other people.

When Anna Mae was a teenager, though, her country-girl life in Nutbush, Tennessee, came to a halt when her parents separated. Floyd eventually made his way to Chicago. And Zelma, along with her two daughters, moved to St. Louis. For Anna Mae, the move to the city was almost like being in a movie, because city life looked like movie life to her.

In St. Louis Anna Mae enrolled in school while Eileen got a job in a hospital. It was difficult for Anna Mae to concentrate on her studies, and soon she was exploring the alternatives that presented themselves in the St. Louis night life. By the time she was seventeen, Anna Mae was allowed to tag along with Eileen when she went out at night.

Anna Mae Bullock on stage with Ike and his band in St. Louis.

The two Bullock girls frequently visited the Club Manhattan, a swanky nightclub in East St. Louis that featured live music. For Anna Mae, the Club Manhattan was just about the most sophisticated place she had ever seen: the women all wore their best dresses and nice jewelry and the men dressed in flashy, dark suits which made them appear to be quite handsome. On her first visit to the Club Manhattan, Anna Mae encountered the first real band that she had ever seen, Ike Turner and his Kings of Rhythm.

IKE'S STORY

The son of a preacher and a seamstress, Ike Turner was born Izear Luster Turner in Clarksdale, Mississippi, on November 5, 1931. As a child during the great American Depression, Ike worked on a chicken farm. The youngster learned to play the piano when a neighbor woman gave him lessons in exchange for chopping wood. By the age of eight, Ike was tired of collecting eggs and began a series of odd jobs, like selling scrap iron, to put extra quarters into his pockets. At one point he even ran away from home to Memphis where he worked as a hallboy in the Hotel Peabody.

Playing music, however, was Ike's main passion. By the time he was 13 years old he quit school to play piano behind such legendary blues musicians as Sonny Boy Williamson, who sang and played a harmonica, and Robert Nighthawk. While he was still a teenager, Ike Turner formed his own band, the Kings of Rhythm.

In 1951 Ike got the opportunity to record a tune that was based on the traditional blues of the early 1950s. The song, titled "Rocket 88," was recorded in Sam Phillips' famous Sun Studios in Memphis, the same studios where Elvis Presley, Jerry Lee Lewis, Roy Orbison, and Johnny Cash later began their recording careers. An earthy jump song that featured the Kings of Rhythm's saxophonist singing the vocals, "Rocket 88" is considered by many historians to be the first rock and roll song ever recorded.

For a short time Ike worked as a studio musician, playing guitar behind such talent as Howlin' Wolf, B.B. King, and Junior Walker. Being a restless young man, Ike quit his job and moved with his band to East St. Louis. He told his former employer that he was going to become a star. In St. Louis, Ike, his common-law wife and two sons, and the Kings of Rhythm all settled in a three-story brick house.

A hard worker who wanted to strike it rich, Ike Turner managed to work out a schedule for his group that allowed them to play three clubs a night. Early in the evening the band would work in the Club Imperial playing the popular songs of the day for white teenagers. They then moved over to a black club at around ten in the evening to play rhythm and blues. Finally, around one in the morning, the Kings of Rhythm ended up at the Club Manhattan to play gritty blues and hard-edged R&B numbers, a great many of which were Ike's original compositions.

IKE AND
TINA TURNER REVUE

After watching Ike Turner's Kings of Rhythm for a few weeks, Anna Mae Bullock talked to the band's leader about getting up on stage and singing. Ike however, was not taken by the scrawny seventeen-year-old and didn't pay much attention to her.

One night the drummer put the microphone down in the audience so that people could sing along. The microphone was handed to Anna Mae's sister, but she refused to sing. "I took the microphone and just started singing — some B.B. King tune, I believe," recalls Tina Turner today. Once she cut loose, everyone in the club came running to see who the girl was.

After the show Ike came around to Anna Mae and said shyly that he didn't know that she could *really* sing. After that, Ike began working the teenager into his stage show whenever he could. Ike went out and bought gowns that sparkled, long white gloves and costume jewelry that the band's new singer could wear on stage. "I felt like I was rich. And it felt good," Tina remembers.

It wasn't much longer before Anna Mae moved into the house where the rest of the band lived. She started spending her time with Raymond Hill, who played saxophone for the band during that time. After she graduated from high school in 1958, Anna Mae and Raymond Hill had a son whom she named Raymond Craig. At this time, Anna Mae and Ike Turner had a relationship that was much like big brother and little sister.

By the time her son was born, Anna Mae was a full, working member of the band. She sang in the St. Louis night clubs every evening and returned home to the three-story house for late night meals of steaks or pork chops. Around 1960, Ike decided that the band should move out to California. Recording the song "Rocket 88" had given Ike a taste of what it was like to make hit singles, and he figured the best place to begin a recording career would be in Los Angeles. Because Ike had been paying more attention to his career and recording sessions than he had to his wife, the pair soon split up. Ike asked Anna Mae to travel with him to California.

Before the trip, Ike wanted to tie up another of his

projects, recording a song he had written titled "A Fool in Love." The plan was to record a demo record — that is, a record whose production is rough and unfinished, but one that gives record companies an idea of the artist's writing and performing talents — and show it to major record companies. Ike had lined up a male to sing the song, but on the day of the recording session, he didn't show up. So Ike asked Anna Mae to sing on the track.

"A Fool in Love," an unpolished R&B number, quickly caught the attention of Juggy Murray, who was the head of Sue Records in New York City. He signed Ike Turner with the record company. The song was released as a single in 1960 under the name of "Ike and Tina Turner." Ike got the idea of "Tina" from an old movie about a jungle queen, and Anna Mae first found out about her new name when she read the credits on the label of the 45.

"A Fool in Love" quickly rose to the top of the national charts, hitting the Number Two position on the R&B charts and entered the Top Thirty on the pop charts. Right away Ike put together another group to tour the country in support of the hit single. The Ike and Tina Turner Revue, as the group was called, included the Ikettes, three women who sang backing vocals. The Revue would drive from town to town playing gigs. Whenever possible, Ike would book a local recording studio in hopes that the band could come up with the next hit single. The pace was exhausting, and the members of the band and the Ikettes changed quite frequently.

WHAT'S LOVE GOT TO DO WITH IT

Ike and Tina Turner got married in 1962 on a weekend trip to Tijuana, Mexico. The couple set up a household in a Los Angeles suburb with Ike, Jr. and Michael, Ike's two sons by his former wife, and Raymond Craig, Tina's son. Shortly thereafter Tina gave birth to Ike's son, Ronnie.

"I was a fun mom, but very strong," Tina told *Good Morning America* during an interview. She was very firm when it came to teaching her sons manners. "I didn't allow them to speak slang. By slang, I mean that hip

25

attitude. I didn't like it, and they knew that wasn't one of their ways of expressing themselves with me." Tina was also concerned about what the boys ate, making sure they had well-balanced meals.

Under Ike's guidance, the hit singles kept coming. "A Fool in Love" was followed by a funky workout called "I Idolize You." Next came the call-and-response "It's Gonna Work Out Fine," then "Poor Fool," "Tra La La La La," and "You Should'a Treated Me Right." All of this recording activity was enough to keep the Ike and Tina Turner Revue on the road for most of the months of the year. And the show they fashioned for the road was a highly choreographed production that resembled a Las Vegas stage act.

In 1965 the Revue was playing at Cyrano's, a club on Sunset Strip in Hollywood, when Phil Spector heard the group. Spector, a world-famous record producer who created the classic wall-of-sound technique by over-dubbing scores of musicians for songs such as "Be My Baby," "Da Doo Ron Ron," "Baby, I Love You," and other early sixties pop songs, was tremendously impressed with Tina's larger-than-life voice.

He approached Ike with the idea of featuring the Revue in a concert movie he was working on, *The Big T.N.T. Show*. Spector was also interested in hearing Tina sing a song he had written with two other songwriters. The song was "River Deep, Mountain High." The basic track for the song was already recorded, and Spector only needed a dynamic female voice to finish it off. Ike struck a bargain with Spector: he could use Tina if he would credit the record to "Ike and Tina Turner" when it was released. Spector agreed to this, and Tina entered the studio with the producer.

Tina, who had not worked with an outside producer by this time, was thrilled to sing for the man who was responsible for making a lot of the hit singles she had

Tina Turner in an uncustomarily quiet pose. She and Ike rarely stopped moving once they had begun turning out hits.

heard on the radio.

The session left a lasting impression on Tina, who had only belted out blues and R&B tunes during her show-biz career. "For the first time in my life, it wasn't R&B. I finally had the chance to *sing*," she remembers. "The material was more like rock and roll, and I've always liked rock and roll."

Released in 1966, "River Deep, Mountain High" wasn't the huge success that Spector imagined it would be. The producer had hoped the song would go to the top of the American charts, but by that time, the type of music that was being played on the radio had shifted to quaint, jingle-jangle rock sounds of the British groups like the Beatles and the Rolling Stones. Tina Turner's version of "River Deep, Mountain High" was one of the last songs that the discouraged Spector produced for a long time.

"River Deep, Mountain High" did, however, become quite the sensation in England and the rest of Europe. Suddenly the Ike and Tina Turner Revue found themselves big stars on the other side of the Atlantic. When the Rolling Stones toured Europe in 1966, the superstar rock group invited Ike and Tina along to open the show.

With the opportunity to play before a large white audience — an audience that had thus far not bought their records — Ike and Tina realized that they had tapped into the current scene. In order to cross further into the mainstream pop market, the Revue worked up their versions of standard rock songs like the Beatles' "Come

Together," the Rolling Stones' "Honky Tonk Woman,"
Sly and the Family Stone's "I Want To Take You Higher,"
and Creedence Clearwater Revival's "Proud Mary,"
which became one of the most popular numbers in the
show. Ike and Tina Turner again toured with the Rolling
Stones when the British band came to the United States
in 1969.

BREAKING UP IS HARD TO DO

Although the hits kept coming, the marriage of Ike and Tina began to sour during all this activity. Tina was no longer in love with Ike; she stuck by his side because, as some of her friends now describe it, she felt loyal to the man who had helped make her a star. And certainly being with the Revue was better than picking fruit and cotton back in Tennessee.

Even though Ike kept tight reins on Tina's activity, she still managed to become involved in projects on her own. Her performance in the 1975 film *Tommy* brought her a lot of attention. Based on a rock opera released in 1969 by the English rock group, the Who, *Tommy* told the story of a deaf, dumb, and blind kid who became a leader for his generation. In the movie Tina played a fortune teller of sorts and sang one song, "Acid Queen." This was Tina's first experience in playing a role in the movies, which was her childhood dream. Her appearance in *The Big T.N.T. Show* didn't count, since it was a concert documentary.

The appearance in *Tommy* helped bring Tina Turner to an even larger rock audience which had never seen her perform on stage. Tina followed up that opportunity with *Acid Queen,* a solo album recorded for United Artists. The album was recorded in the studio Ike had built near the Turners' Baldwin Hills home in southern California. Although Tina covered such rock songs as the Who's "I Can See for Miles" and Led Zeppelin's "Whole Lotta Love," the primitive R&B arrangements Ike created for the material did not appeal to the mainstream market, and the record didn't sell well.

By this point Ike and Tina were constantly arguing and fighting. Ike was known to hit his wife, and a number of times she was forced to appear on stage with makeup covering bruises and black eyes. During a 1975 tour with the Revue, the fighting became too intense for Tina to handle any longer. Once the tour group was settled in their hotel rooms in Dallas, Tina decided it would be better for her if she were on her own, away from the abuse and neglect of her husband. When Ike was asleep in the hotel, Tina walked out and caught a plane back to Los Angeles. She had only thirty-six cents in her handbag.

THE ROAD BACK

For the first year after Tina Turner left her husband, she did nothing. She stayed with friends and didn't perform on stage. Someone introduced her to Buddhism, and she became interested in that religion's form of meditation. "Spiritually it really helped me find out what I was going to do next," she says.

Eventually she came to the realization that she had to work, and the only thing that she knew how to do was to sing on stage. Because she had walked out on Ike in the middle of a tour, the remaining dates of that tour had to be canceled. Unfortunately the promoters who lost money from that tour sued Tina for the damages, and she had to raise thousands of dollars to pay them back.

A friend in the recording industry agreed to help Tina. He steered her into performing on the lounge circuit, appearing at hotels in Las Vegas and Lake Tahoe. The shows may not have been what Tina would have preferred to do, but the pay was very good, and it was a way of getting herself out of debt.

There were not too many people at that time who believed that Tina Turner would amount to much after leaving the Revue. Her career up until then had been completely molded by Ike, from her name to the songs she sang to the costumes she wore on stage. In fact, the show that Tina took on the road alone was not much different from the one she had performed with Ike and the Revue. She sang "Proud Mary," "River Deep, Mountain High," and had a trio of women singers backing her up. The show seemed like an "oldies" show performed by a singer recycling her greatest hits. Even the members of the band she hired to back her up felt that Tina Turner would probably perform for a couple of years doing her old songs and then fade from the scene.

But Tina believed in herself and wasn't ashamed to be playing the lounge shows in the resort hotels. Realizing that her strongest market was in Europe, where Ike and Tina had been big stars, she took her small band to the continent and played the clubs of major cities. If her solo career was to take off she would need a hit record, she began to look around for a producer. Initially she met with Richard Perry, the man who had produced hit records for the Pointer Sisters and Diana Ross. But the sessions that resulted from her involvement with Perry were not very exceptional, and an album was never released.

"I am hard to capture on tape," Tina has said. Singing alone in the studio with a pair of headphones on it is difficult for a performer to generate the type of excitement that a crowd of people inspires, and Tina feels that her best performances have always been in concert. "I don't know if my best was *ever* captured on tape," she has said.

In 1980 Tina began to look around for a manager. She wanted someone who would believe in her potential as a major entertainer in the same way that she did and someone who wouldn't chuckle at her when she expressed her secret desire to develop her acting career. She decided she needed a manager who had worked with someone else who combined a singing career with an acting career. When Tina looked at Olivia Newton-John's career, it seemed to her that the singer/actress had the best deal possible. She had hit records, and in between the records, she performed in popular movies. So Tina Turner sent an invitation to Olivia's management, requesting their presence when she was to appear at the Fairmont Hotel in San Francisco.

During her comeback to a solo career, Tina's concerts looked more like Las Vegas shows—but her energy and voice still made them memorable.

Tina's show consisted of disco-ized versions of her songs and featured glitzy, sequined outfits more suited to a Las Vegas stage than to a rock arena. The management team saw potential in Tina's act but decided not to sign her. There was, however, an assistant in the management team named Roger Davies who liked Tina quite a lot. Davies was looking to start his own management company, and Tina was perfect for him. Once the two joined forces, they began to map out an entirely new phase of Tina's career, one that would take her out of the lounges and on to the major rock stages and, finally, into the movies.

To begin with, Davies set about updating Tina's act. He kept in her strong material like "River Deep, Mountain High" and "Proud Mary" but deleted some of the older R&B songs. Davies also saw to it that Tina returned to Europe, a place where she had remained a big star.

PRIVATE DANCER

While in Europe, Tina was approached by the members of Heaven 17, a British synthesizer group, to perform on a studio project. The song turned out to be an updated version of an old Temptations song, "Ball of Confusion." Tina was familiar with the song, but the arrangement that Heaven 17 had concocted, a rhythmic synthesizer track, was a much more contemporary sound than hers. It was the beginning of something new for Tina.

"The sound, the beat — it was *today*. It was the direction I was interested in moving in," Tina said later. "It felt good to hear my voice on something so contemporary."

A year later, in 1983, Roger Davies had secured a recording contract with the English division of Capitol Records. Aware of the singer's continued popularity in Europe, the company decided to give Tina a chance. In between gigs in the nightclubs, Tina again entered the studio with the members of Heaven 17 to record some new music. For her comeback single the producers settled upon an old R&B tune by Al Green called "Let's Stay Together." It was ironic that this particular song was chosen, because Tina wanted something modern and in the rock vein. Yet in the end they settled on a very familiar rhythm and blues song.

When it was released in England, "Let's Stay Together" quickly rose to the Top Ten on the charts. Suddenly the woman who nobody thought would amount to anything on her own had a huge hit single on her hands. The demand for her to tour again in Europe was tremendous. Capitol Records, who initially had taken only a passing interest in the artist, decided to release the single in the United States where it again surprised everyone by reaching Number Five on the R&B charts and Number One on the dance charts.

This resounding success prompted Tina's record company to request an entire album of material from the singer. The only problem was that the company wanted the record to be completed in two weeks, and

Tina was in the middle of another of her European tours. With the help of Roger Davies and the men from Heaven 17, songs were selected, musicians hired, and arrangements worked out in the studio for the album that would become the historic, Grammy-winning *Private Dancer*.

One of the songs that had been offered to Tina almost didn't make it onto the album. "What's Love Got to Do with It," a ballad by an Australian guitar player, didn't meet with her approval. "It didn't sound like me," Tina said about the song the first time she heard it. But she met with the songwriter, and he told her that he could tailor the song to her style. He then played the song on the guitar with a slight reggae beat to it. Still not convinced that the song was as great as everyone else thought it was, Tina decided to record it anyway.

When it was released in 1984, "What's Love Got to Do with It" rose to the top of the American pop charts and became Tina Turner's first Number One single. By the time she started touring the big arenas in the United States as the opening act for Lionel Richie, there was no doubt that little Anna Mae of Nutbush, Tennessee, would become one of the hottest acts in show business. *Private Dancer* produced four hit singles — "What's Love Got to Do with It," "Better Be Good To Me," "Let's Stay Together," and "Private Dancer."

TINA TURNER: SUPERSTAR

In the fall of 1984 Tina caught a flight to Australia to work with the film director on her first dramatic film role, that of Auntie Entity in *Mad Max Beyond Thunderdome*. By now, Tina had filmed a number of videos for her songs, but acting in a movie was far different than pretending she was singing one of her songs for a video camera. A science fiction movie about people living off the land after a nuclear war, *Beyond Thunderdome* needed an attractive villainess to play opposite the lead character. In the movie Tina wore a long white wig and dresses made out of chain. She also sang two songs for the movie, "One of the Living" and "We Don't Need Another Hero."

Tina's superstar status was confirmed when she was invited to participate in the benefit recording session that produced the single "We Are the World." The money

Tina sparkles with energy in concert. Working up a sweat on stage is still her only exercise, but she stays in top shape.

raised from the single was used to help feed the people who were dying of starvation in Africa. On July 13, 1985, two "Live Aid" concerts were arranged, one in England and one in the United States. Over 50 recording artists performed during the day, and the concert sites were linked together by satellite connections.

At the end of the day, Tina Turner came on stage to sing a duet with Mick Jagger, lead singer of the Rolling Stones, in front of 90,000 people in the JFK Stadium. The pair sang "State of Shock," a song Mick sang with Michael Jackson on the *Victory* album, and "It's Only Rock 'n' Roll," a classic Rolling Stones song. It was nearly two decades earlier that Ike and Tina had opened the show for Mick Jagger and the other Rolling Stones. This time, however, Tina Turner wasn't the supporting act — she was the star.

Tina appeared in *Mad Max Beyond Thunderdome* as villainess Auntie Entity, and finally launched her dream career: acting.